IF YOU'RE NOT LAUGHING, YOU'RE LOSING: THE ATHLETE'S GUIDE TO USING HUMOR AS A HIGH-PERFORMANCE MINDSET TOOL

By Erin Herle, M.S., CMPC

INTRODUCTION
"If You're Not Laughing, You're Losing"
WHY THIS BOOK EXISTS
CHAPTER 1: WHY HUMOR WORKS (AND WHY YOU NEED IT)
"Your Brain Is an Asshole"
1. Humor Shuts Down Overthinking
Your brain loves to catastrophize.
2. Humor Reduces Stress & Keeps You Loose
CHAPTER 2: THE P.L.A.Y. FRAMEWORK
How to Weaponize Humor So You Stop Taking Yourself Too Seriously and Start Performing Better
The P.L.A.Y. Framework
P - Perspective Shift: Reframing Pressure with Humor
L - Loosen Up: Using Humor to Regulate Stress
A - Adaptive Confidence: Handling Mistakes with Humor
Y - Yes, And: Committing to the Bit (Even When It Feels Dumb)
Wrapping Up the P.L.A.Y. Framework
CHAPTER 3: APPLYING HUMOR IN REAL COMPETITION
How to Trick Your Brain into Performing Under Pressure Without Self-Destructing
Pre-Competition: Breaking the Nerve Spiral
During Competition: Staying Loose & Focused
After Competition: Processing Without Spiraling
CHAPTER 4: TRAINING HUMOR LIKE A SKILL
How to Stop Taking Yourself Too Seriously While Still Taking Your Sport Seriously
1. Make Humor a Habit
2. Integrate Humor Into Training
3. Test Humor Under Pressure
4. Start Small, Stay Consistent
CHAPTER 5: PUTTING IT ALL TOGETHER
How to Stop Letting Stress Win and Start Playing Like You Actually Enjoy This Sport

1. Before Competition

2. During Competition

3. After Competition

Final Game Plan:

Final Words:

PRINTABLE SUMMARY: THE P.L.A.Y. FRAMEWORK CHEAT SHEET

About the Author

INTRODUCTION

"If You're Not Laughing, You're Losing"

Picture this: You're standing in the bullpen before a big match. Your hands are sweaty, your heart is racing, and you're trying to act like you're *totally fine* even though your brain is screaming,*What if I forget everything I've ever learned and just collapse into a fetal position on the mat?*

At that moment, you have two choices:

1. **Spiral into an anxiety vortex** and overanalyze your entire life.
2. **Laugh at the ridiculousness of your brain trying to kill you when all you're doing is a sport you voluntarily signed up for.**

The truth is, **athletes take themselves too seriously.** And yeah, I get it—winning matters, competition is intense, and you don't want to look like an idiot in front of everyone. But here's what no one tells you:

> **The athletes who stay loose, adaptable, and can laugh at themselves under pressure tend to perform better than the ones who act like they're storming Normandy every time they compete.**

Because humor isn't just about making things "fun." It's a psychological weapon. A performance enhancer. A way to shut down the panic spiral and stay sharp when it counts.

This isn't about being funny. It's about not freezing when the pressure hits.

In this book, I'm going to show you how to use humor **intentionally**—not just as a way to crack jokes in the locker room, but as an actual mental skill that will help you:

- **Regulate stress and anxiety before competition**
- **Bounce back from mistakes without spiraling into self-loathing**
- **Focus without turning into a robot devoid of joy**
- **Build confidence without being a delusional narcissist**
- **Actually enjoy competing instead of feeling like you're walking to your own execution**

I'm going to break down the science, the strategy, and the **real-world ways you can use humor to get out of your own head and into the moment.**

And don't worry—I'm not about to hit you with some "laughter is the best medicine" fluff. This isn't a corporate wellness seminar. **This is about learning how to weaponize humor for performance, resilience, and winning.**

WHY THIS BOOK EXISTS

I didn't write this because I think humor is cute. I wrote it because I've lived the anxiety spiral, and I've coached enough athletes to know they're tired of being told to "just breathe" or "stay positive" when their insides feel like a battlefield.

This book exists because too many athletes are grinding themselves into the ground with no mental tools other than white-knuckling it and hoping it doesn't all fall apart under pressure.

Humor became one of the most effective tools I used—not just personally, but with my clients. And not because we were trying to make light of serious situations. Quite the opposite. Humor helped us face the serious stuff without collapsing under the weight of it.

This book is for the overthinkers, the perfectionists, the high-achievers who feel like they have to earn the right to be calm.

If you've ever felt like your brain is your biggest opponent— you're not alone. This is your permission to stop taking yourself so seriously... and start training your mind in a way that actually works.

Let's get into it.

CHAPTER 1: WHY HUMOR WORKS (AND WHY YOU NEED IT)

"Your Brain Is an Asshole"

Your brain, despite all its advanced functions, **is not actually on your side when it comes to high-pressure situations.** It evolved for survival, not competition.

Which means that when you're about to compete, it doesn't say:

> *"Ah yes, time to access all my hard-earned training and execute with precision!"*

Nope. Instead, it throws out:

> *"Holy shit, we're gonna die. Do anything but remain calm and logical."*

This is your **stress response** kicking in. Your nervous system is trying to "help" by making you hyper-alert, but instead, it just turns you into an over-caffeinated raccoon with existential dread.

And that's where humor comes in.

> **Humor is a psychological reset button.** It takes your brain out of panic mode and back into a state where you can actually function.

Here's why it works:

1. Humor Shuts Down Overthinking

Your brain loves to **catastrophize.**

- "What if I lose?"
- "What if I embarrass myself?"
- "What if my opponent is secretly an Olympic gold medalist disguised as a normal human?"

Humor interrupts that spiral. It forces your brain to shift gears, **reframing fear as something absurd instead of something life-threatening.**

Example:
You're a BJJ competitor, freaking out before a match. Instead of spiraling, you think:

> *"Worst-case scenario? I get choked unconscious, wake up, and think I won."*

Suddenly, it's **not so serious anymore.** You've given yourself permission to relax, and now your body can do what it's trained to do.

2. Humor Reduces Stress & Keeps You Loose

Tension is the enemy of performance. Every coach on earth preaches **relaxation**, but telling someone to "just relax" is about as effective as telling a toddler to stop crying.

Laughter is a physiological hack for relaxation.

It **lowers cortisol, increases dopamine, and literally resets your nervous system.** This is why you see elite athletes joking around before competition—it's not just for show. It's a **deliberate way to keep their bodies loose and their minds sharp.**

3. Humor Increases Confidence (Without The Ego)

Confidence isn't about believing you'll never fail. It's about believing that if you do, **you'll be fine.** Humor is a shortcut to that mindset.

When you can laugh at yourself, mistakes don't feel like **identity-shattering tragedies.** They're just moments. And when you're **not terrified of failing, you perform better.**

Example:
A fighter who can joke, *"Well, at least I lasted longer than last time"* after a tough match is already in a better mindset than the guy crying in the locker room.

CHAPTER 2: THE P.L.A.Y. FRAMEWORK

How to Weaponize Humor So You Stop Taking Yourself Too Seriously and Start Performing Better

Alright, now that we've established that humor isn't just for comedians and weird uncles, it's time to turn it into an actual performance tool. Enter:

The P.L.A.Y. Framework

(Because what's an effective mental model without an unnecessary acronym?)

Each letter represents a trainable skill that makes humor a performance enhancer, not just a personality trait.

P - Perspective Shift: Reframing Pressure With Humor

Humor interrupts catastrophic thinking and replaces it with absurdity. It shifts your mindset from fear to curiosity, and from panic to presence.

How to Train It:

"Find the Funny" Thought Reframe: Take a stress-inducing situation and rewrite it as a comedy bit. One sprinter told me she reimagined her starting block routine as the opening of an action movie where the stakes were a sandwich, not a gold medal.

Personify Your Inner Doubt: Turn self-doubt into a ridiculous character or voice. One jiu-jitsu competitor gave her inner critic the persona of a passive-aggressive aunt who says things like, "Oh honey, you're trying your best, bless your heart." It helped her recognize unhelpful thoughts faster—and let them go.

L - Loosen Up: Using Humor To Regulate Stress

You play better when you're loose. Humor helps reset your nervous system and counteract tension.

How to Train It:

Pre-Game Humor Ritual: One volleyball player brings a small rubber chicken to warmups. Not because it's magical, but because it reminds her not to clench like she's auditioning for a Marvel role.

Humor-Based Breathing Reset: Pair breathwork with silly imagery. A wrestler imagines exhaling a balloon animal shaped like his anxiety. "It floats away wearing a cowboy hat." Works every time.

A - Adaptive Confidence: Handling Mistakes With Humor

Humor builds emotional flexibility. It helps you bounce back from mistakes without falling into a shame spiral.

How to Train It:

Failure Bingo: Create a bingo card of minor, ridiculous things that could go wrong. One swimmer had things like "goggles fill with water" and "forgot flip-turn, freestyle somersault instead." Afterward, she laughed and checked off half the card.

Delusional Athlete Interview: Do a fake post-match interview with exaggerated confidence. A judo athlete once said, "The fall? Oh yes, that was interpretive. I call it tactical poetry."

Y - Yes, And: Committing To The Bit (Even When It Feels Dumb)

Yes, And is a mindset. It's about staying open to whatever happens and responding with presence rather than panic. Borrowed from improv comedy, it teaches athletes how to roll with mistakes instead of shutting down.

How to Train It:

Yes, And Recovery Drill: When something goes wrong in training or competition, say "Yes, and…" and follow it with your next action. Example: "Yes, I just got passed… and now I'll frame and recover like a maniac."

Deliberate Ridiculousness: Try warming up with exaggerated or silly movement—not to be a clown, but to remind yourself that you don't need to be perfect to be effective.

Mini Improv Challenge: In solo practice, give yourself a goofy constraint and find a way to make it work: "Yes, I must shadowbox like a penguin for 30 seconds… and still stay focused."

This mindset trains your brain to adapt with curiosity instead of freezing in frustration.

Wrapping Up The P.L.A.Y. Framework

The P.L.A.Y. Framework isn't about pretending your sport is easy or your goals don't matter. It's about approaching pressure with flexibility, not fear. Humor helps you regulate stress, stay grounded, and keep moving even when everything feels chaotic.

Use P.L.A.Y. to:

- Reframe what's hard (Perspective Shift)

- Relax when you're tense (Loosen Up)

- Bounce back after failure (Adaptive Confidence)

- Stay engaged when things go sideways (Yes, And)

When you train humor the way you train technique, it becomes a high-performance tool—not just a coping mechanism, but part of your competitive edge.

So the next time your brain starts taking things too seriously, remember: you're not fragile, you're just overdue for a laugh.

CHAPTER 3: APPLYING HUMOR IN REAL COMPETITION

How to Trick Your Brain into Performing Under Pressure Without Self-Destructing

Humor can be used at every stage of competition to keep you present, adaptable, and emotionally regulated. This chapter gives you real strategies *and* some context for what it looks like in action.

One of my jiu-jitsu clients, a purple belt, struggled with being assertive. She'd freeze during transitions or hesitate when breaking grips. Her body knew what to do, but her brain kept asking for permission.

We worked on a cue she could use mid-roll to snap her out of it. She landed on: "No, motherfucker." Simple, sharp, and hers.

At her next comp, she got stuck in closed guard and felt the panic rising. Then that voice kicked in—"No, motherfucker." She smirked, stood up, broke the guard, and got to work.

That one phrase reminded her she belonged there. It helped her stop asking and start acting.

Pre-Competition: Breaking The Nerve Spiral

How to Use It:

- **Worst-Case Bingo**: Write five absurd possible outcomes and get a point if any happen. One athlete I worked with, a high school wrestler, once wrote, "Singlet rips in front of entire gym." It didn't happen, but just imagining it got him to loosen up before walking to the mat.

- **Self-Roast Pep Talk**: Replace dramatic self-talk with light, silly self-commentary. A swimmer I worked with used to whisper, "Don't false start, don't false start," until she started saying, "Hey feet, try not to betray me today." Way more effective.

- **Pre-Game Comedy Clip**: Watch a funny video to lower tension. A jiu-jitsu athlete told me she always watched a clip of a cat trying to fight its reflection before walking into the bullpen. "It reminds me that I'm not the only one battling imaginary enemies."

During Competition: Staying Loose & Focused

How to Use It:

- **Cue Word Comedy**: Use funny focus phrases (e.g., "unleash the chaos gremlin"). A basketball player replaced "stay low" with "be a gremlin" and it snapped her out of robotic movement every time.

- **Post-Mistake One-Liner**: Reset after mistakes with a short, funny comment. One athlete actually whispered "nailed it" every time she missed a shot. It kept her cool and focused for the next play.

- **Secret Smirk**: Smirk on purpose to trick your nervous system into calm. One track athlete told me he practiced smirking at the start line—not because he thought he was cool, but because it reminded him not to clench like a brick wall.

After Competition: Processing Without Spiraling

How to Use It:

- **Delusional Press Conference**: Pretend you're being interviewed post-competition and exaggerate. A tennis player recorded a mock interview where she said, "Yes, I lost, but that backhand into the net? A masterpiece of misdirection."

- **Highlight Reel of Shame**: Make fun of your own errors with dramatic music or commentary. A volleyball team edited together their bloopers with slow motion and "Titanic" music. Not only did they bond over it, but it helped them reflect without shame.

- **Preposterous Awards Ceremony**: Hand out ridiculous "awards" to lighten the mood. A group of cross-country runners gave out things like "Best Effort to Pretend the Cramp Wasn't That Bad" and "Loudest Breath Soundtrack."

Apply one strategy from each phase, and let humor become a consistent, reliable part of your mental routine., and let humor become a consistent, reliable part of your mental routine.

CHAPTER 4: TRAINING HUMOR LIKE A SKILL

How to Stop Taking Yourself Too Seriously While Still Taking Your Sport Seriously

You train technique. You train strength. It's time to train humor, too.

Most athletes think of humor as something that just "happens"—something you either have or you don't. But like anything else in performance, humor is a tool. It can be sharpened, practiced, and embedded into your routine so it shows up when you need it the most.

This chapter is about building consistency. It's about giving yourself the space to play on purpose—not as a break from training, but as a way to train your mind right alongside your body.

1. Make Humor A Habit

You can't expect to magically laugh your way out of a chokehold if you haven't trained your brain to access playfulness when it's stressed. Start building humor into your daily rhythm.

Daily Dumb Thought: Write down one absurd, exaggerated, or ironic thought a day. Keep a running list in your phone or notebook. Example: "If I train hard enough today, I might unlock a hidden jiu-jitsu cheat code."

Humor Anchor: Find your go-to meme, gif, video, or quote that always makes you laugh. Use it as a reset button on high-stress days. Athletes have told me they keep folders titled "In Case of Emergency, Laugh."

Reframe Something Annoying: Got a parking ticket? Call it a donation to your city's infrastructure. Forgot your water bottle? You're training like it's 1993—raw and dehydrated. Silly reframes shift your perspective and keep stress from snowballing.

The point isn't to deny reality. It's to defuse the emotional tension that comes with it.

2. Integrate Humor Into Training

If you want humor to show up on game day, you have to invite it to practice.

- **Worst-Case Scenario Training:** During drills, imagine outrageous outcomes. "What if I shoot for a double leg and end up hugging them into a draw?" Making mistakes playful removes their sting and increases adaptability.

- **Silent Comedy Challenge:** Do an entire warm-up or drill round in exaggerated mime style—huge facial expressions, pantomime reactions. It's ridiculous and fun, but it also improves body awareness and reduces tension.

- **Meme the Technique:** After a tough practice, take a photo or video of a failed technique and caption it like a meme. "When you almost remember the counter but end up spooning your opponent." Bonus: You'll actually remember what went wrong.

Training doesn't need to be a grind to be effective. In fact, a little laughter often leads to more reps, better retention, and fewer injuries caused by tension or burnout.

3. Test Humor Under Pressure

The real magic happens when you bring humor into competition and scrimmages. This is where the reps start to pay off.

- **Pre-Game Humor Strategy:** Choose one ritual you use to get grounded—comedy clips, a one-liner, a self-roast in the mirror. Example: "This is your big moment, buddy. Try not to trip walking in."

- **Mid-Game Reset:** Plan a cue word or visual that makes you smirk and re-center. One client visualized a cartoon version of themselves doing exactly what they just messed up—and it made the next rep smoother.

- **Post-Game Humor Review:** After a match, recap your most absurd moment like you're on SportsCenter. Give yourself a fake award. "Best Supporting Role in a Dramatic Dive."

If you can laugh, you can reflect. If you can reflect, you can improve.

4. Start Small, Stay Consistent

You don't have to overhaul your mindset overnight. Start by choosing one humor strategy from each category:

- Daily Habit: One laugh-worthy thought or reframe.

- Training Integration: One playful twist to a drill.

- Competition Practice: One cue for calm under pressure.

Build it like you would any skill: deliberately, consistently, and with a little room for failure (and jokes about that failure).

Over time, humor becomes a performance enhancer—not just

something you do when you're winning, but something that helps you stay in the game no matter what happens.

Because your sport is serious. But you don't have to be humorless to take it seriously.

CHAPTER 5: PUTTING IT ALL TOGETHER

How to Stop Letting Stress Win and Start Playing Like You Actually Enjoy This Sport

You've got the tools. Now it's time to use them—not just occasionally, but consistently, so humor becomes part of your athletic DNA.

1. Before Competition

Use humor to interrupt nerves and get present.

This is where most athletes start losing before they even step on the mat, field, court, or stage. They think themselves into stress paralysis. But humor is a pattern breaker.

Worst-case bingo: Take those doomsday thoughts and turn them into a game. Laugh at the part of you that thinks your shoelace coming untied mid-match equals the end of your career.

Self-roast pep talk: Replace the "I have to win" speech with "Let's try not to spontaneously combust today." It's cheeky, but it diffuses pressure instantly.

Pre-game comedy clip: Start collecting your go-to videos. Make a playlist called "Competitive Edge (But Funny)" and hit play when you're tying your belt or lacing your shoes.

2. During Competition

Use humor to reset quickly and stay adaptable.

Once the action starts, you're going to make mistakes. It's inevitable. What matters is whether you panic... or play through.

Funny cue words: Choose phrases that snap you back into your body without sounding like a military command. "Gremlin mode engaged" beats "Be aggressive."

One-liner mistake recovery: One of my clients whispered "Bold strategy" every time they messed up. It made their coach laugh and instantly dropped the tension.

Secret smirk: Smirking isn't arrogance—it's strategy. It tells your nervous system, "We're okay. We're still in this."

3. After Competition

Use humor to review and learn without spiraling.

This is where humor becomes growth fuel. Reflection doesn't have to feel like punishment.

Delusional press conference: What would your over-the-top alter ego say after that match? Channel them.

Highlight reel of shame: Seriously, edit a reel with dramatic music. You'll see how survivable—and hilarious—your "failures" really are.

Ridiculous team/player awards: "Most Unexpected Faceplant" or "Champion of Accidental Acrobatic Escapes" can help your team process with levity.

Final Game Plan:

Choose one strategy from each phase. Start small and build from there.

Make humor part of your routine, not just your recovery.

Share the practice. Invite teammates, coaches, and training partners into it. It spreads.

Final Words:

The best athletes don't just train hard—they learn how to stay human under pressure. Humor keeps you curious, creative, and courageous. It connects you to your body, your people, and the moment.

Don't let pressure steal your joy. Let humor keep your feet on the ground and your mind in the game.

Now go compete like someone who loves their sport.

PRINTABLE SUMMARY: THE P.L.A.Y. FRAMEWORK CHEAT SHEET

Use this quick-reference tool before training, competition, or recovery.

P — Perspective Shift

Reframe pressure with absurdity

Personify your inner critic

Rewrite worst-case scenarios as comedy bits

L — Loosen Up

Use humor rituals (props, routines)

Pair breathing with silly imagery

Over-exaggerate movement to shake off tension

A — Adaptive Confidence

Bounce back from failure with laughter

Do mock pressers or "bold strategy" one-liners

Normalize mistakes—then move on

Y — Yes, And

Respond with curiosity, not control

Accept what happened—add action, not avoidance

Try improv-style drills (e.g. penguin shadowboxing)

Pick one tool from each letter before competition.

Use it. Reflect on it. Adjust it.

Laugh through it.

ABOUT THE AUTHOR

Erin Herle is a Certified Mental Performance Consultant (CMPC), international-level Brazilian Jiu Jitsu black belt, speaker, and writer. She works with athletes across all sports—but especially loves helping the high-achieving, overthinking, anxiety-prone ones.

She earned her master's degree in sport and performance psychology while training full-time, coaching, and launching a mental health nonprofit. She's competed on some of the biggest stages in combat sports and has experienced both the weight of pressure and the power of play firsthand.

Erin relocated from Los Angeles to Niagara Falls, where she lives with her husband and is still learning how to rest on purpose. Her work blends emotional intelligence, performance psychology, and humor as real mental training—not fluff.

You can find more from Erin at erinherle.com or on Instagram @erinherle.

Manufactured by Amazon.ca
Bolton, ON